Alissa's Hand Lettering Book: Summon Your Creativity with My How-To Lettering and Calligraphy Book with Practice Pages

Copyright © 2017 by E Marie

ALL RIGHTS RESERVED. By purchase of this book, you have been licensed one copy for personal use only. No part of this work may be reproduced, redistributed, or used in any form or by any means without prior written permission of the publisher and copyright owner.

INTRO

Thank you for buying this book! You are on your way to learning a new skill that could be the start of a new career, a new hobby, or just plain fun. This book is a simple and easy to use guide to help you practice the basic shapes and strokes involved in hand-lettering. This an informational tool in a workbook style so you can start your practice today! Please be sure to read and practice every step as we all know that the only way to get better at anything is to practice, practice, practice!

HISTORY

The art of "Hand-lettering" has its roots in the ancient cave drawings of our ancestors and has been developed over thousands of years with the creation of letterforms to represent language. Classic calligraphy using a broad stroke pen was used in the Middle Ages up until Medieval times and fell out of favor around the 20th century. However, Calligraphy and Hand-lettering as an artform is making a huge comeback. Today, Modern Calligraphy is a combination of the classic brushstrokes from centuries ago, comibined with the artist's own personal flair.

USES

There are two fonts we are going to practice in this book; a Modern Calligraphy style font, which is a cursive style font, and a Traditional Calligraphy style font, which is based on the original calligraphy styles of the Middle Ages. These are just two versions of thousands of different ways to write letters. After you are confident with these two forms you may go on to practice others or even design one for yourself. Once you perfect your craft, there are many opportunites for careers in Hand-lettering. Modern Calligraphers or Hand-lettering Artists have careers that range from Graphic Designers, to Typographers, to Custom Sign Painters on buildings and for signs used in Advertising. So pick up your pen and see where it takes you!

SUPPLIES

Hand-lettering can be done with a number of different pens and markers including a traditional steel-head dip pen used in traditional calligraphy and a regular paintbrush for the modern hand-lettering. However, for our practice, we are going to use a brush pen for the Modern font and a chisel-tip calligraphy marker for the Traditional font. Brush pens are basically markers where the tip is shaped and feels like the head of a paintbrush. They come in many different sizes and range from soft to hard. The larger the marker the bigger the letters so I recommend a medium sized brush head with a medium softness for beginners. For the chisel tip marker, try to find a "2.0" in size. As you continue your practice, feel free to play around with different options until you find the one that works for you!

FORM

The secret to mastering any new skill is learning the proper form from the start. Make sure you are sitting in a comfortable position with your writing arm at a 90° angle and your wrist straight. **Brush Pen**: Using the brush pen for the Modern font, hold the pen as you would any other writing object, but rotate your *entire arm including your wrist* ever so slightly to the right if you write with your right and vice-versa for the left. The head of the pen should be at a slight angle when it hits the paper. When moving the pen down and then up across the paper you want to move your entire arm with the pen, not just your wrist. You can do this by keeping your wrist striaght and not bent in either direction. For a thick brushstroke, also referred to as a broadstroke, press down on the pen on the downstroke. For a thin or hairline stroke, lightly kiss the paper with the tip of the pen on the upstroke as you gently lift the pen off the paper. To remember this you can think "Press - Down. Lift - Up." **Chisel tip Marker:** Using the chisel tip marker, follow the same form as above, however, rotate the head the of marker until it is 45 degrees when it hits the paper. Keep the pen at this angle at all times! You will notice that this will give you a thick stroke on the downstroke and a thinner stroke on the upstroke and side strokes. Pay attention to the direction of the strokes when writing each letter! If this doesn't come easy to you, remember to practice practice practice! Your work will improve with the proper form.

BASIC PARTS IN TYPOGRAPHY

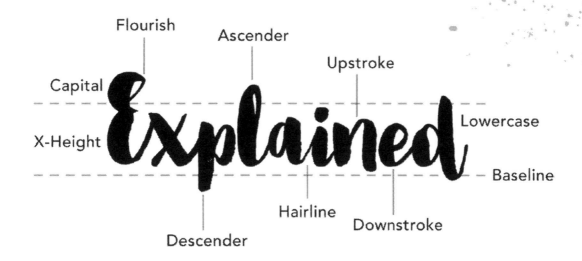

ASCENDER - The part of a lowercase letter that extends above the base
BASELINE - The imaginary line upon which a line of text rests
CAPITAL - A letter of the alphabet that differs in size, specifically height, from its corresponding lowercase letter, in that it is larger and taller.
DESCENDER - The part of a lowercase letter that extends below the base
DOWNSTROKE - A downward stroke made by a pen
FLOURISH - A waving movement, or an extra decoration on a letter
HAIRLINE - The thinnest line of a letter, commonly the upstroke in hand-lettering
LOWERCASE - A letter of the alphabet that differs in size, specifically height, from its corresponding uppercase letter, in that it is smaller and shorter.
UPSTROKE - An upward stroke made by a pen
X-HEIGHT - The height of lowercase letters in a font based on the height of the lowercase letter x

LABEL THE WORD BELOW USING YOUR VOCAB WORDS

MODERN CALLIGRAPHY FONT - CAPITAL LETTERS

A B C D E F G H I
J K L M N O P Q
R S T U V W X Y Z

MODERN CALLIGRAPHY FONT - LOWERCASE LETTERS

a b c d e f g h i
j k l m n o p q r
s t u v w x y z

LET'S PRACTICE! TRACE THE FIRST ROW THEN TRY ON YOUR OWN

LET'S PRACTICE! TRACE THE FIRST ROW THEN TRY ON YOUR OWN

LET'S PRACTICE! TRACE THE FIRST ROW THEN TRY ON YOUR OWN

LET'S PRACTICE! TRACE THE FIRST ROW THEN TRY ON YOUR OWN

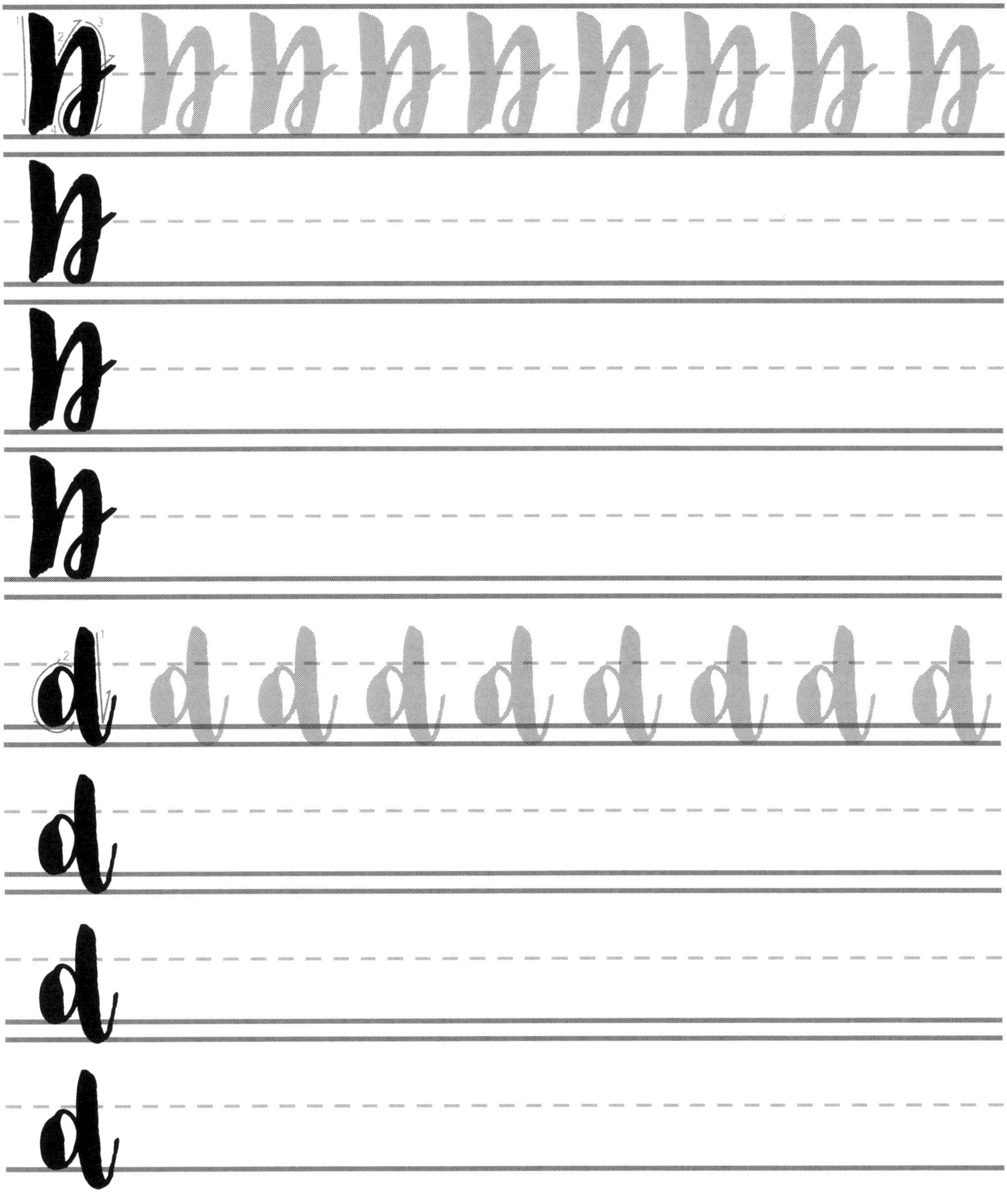

LET'S PRACTICE! TRACE THE FIRST ROW THEN TRY ON YOUR OWN

LET'S PRACTICE! TRACE THE FIRST ROW THEN TRY ON YOUR OWN

LET'S PRACTICE! TRACE THE FIRST ROW THEN TRY ON YOUR OWN

LET'S PRACTICE! TRACE THE FIRST ROW THEN TRY ON YOUR OWN

LET'S PRACTICE! TRACE THE FIRST ROW THEN TRY ON YOUR OWN

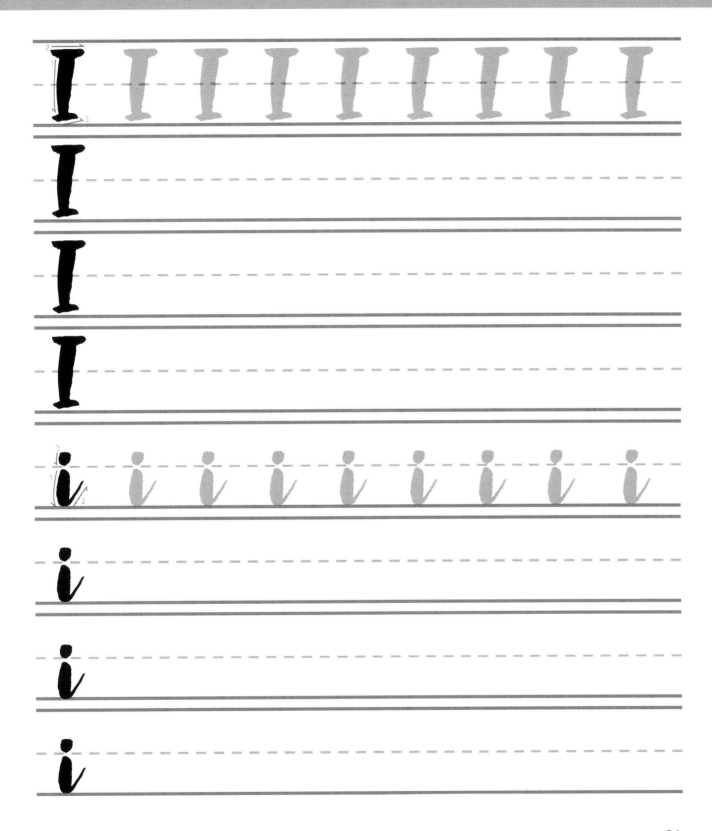

LET'S PRACTICE! TRACE THE FIRST ROW THEN TRY ON YOUR OWN

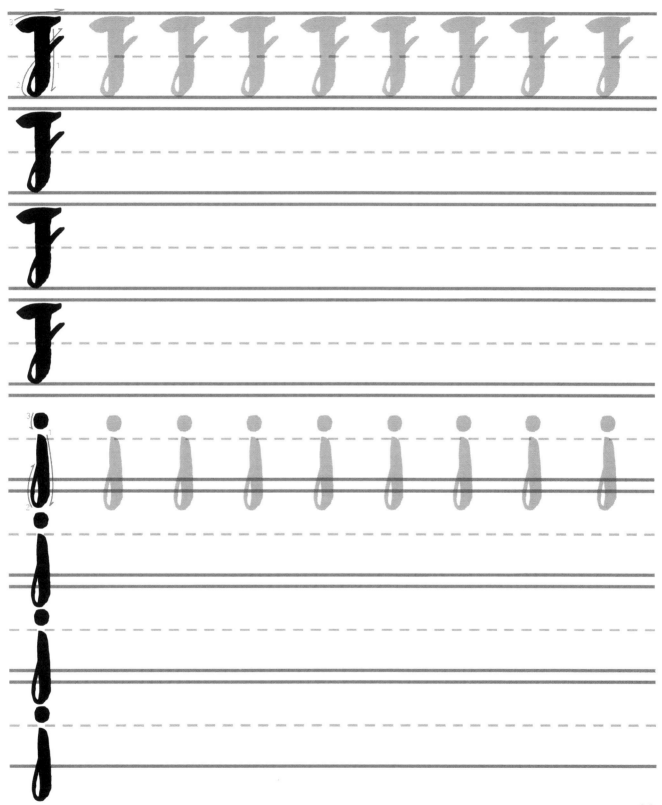

LET'S PRACTICE! TRACE THE FIRST ROW THEN TRY ON YOUR OWN

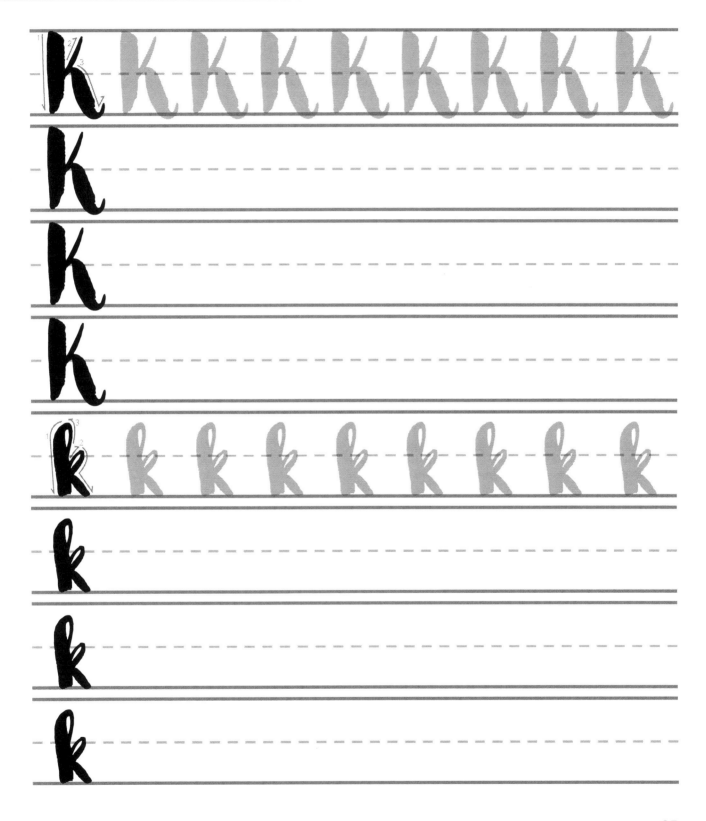

LET'S PRACTICE! TRACE THE FIRST ROW THEN TRY ON YOUR OWN

LET'S PRACTICE! TRACE THE FIRST ROW THEN TRY ON YOUR OWN

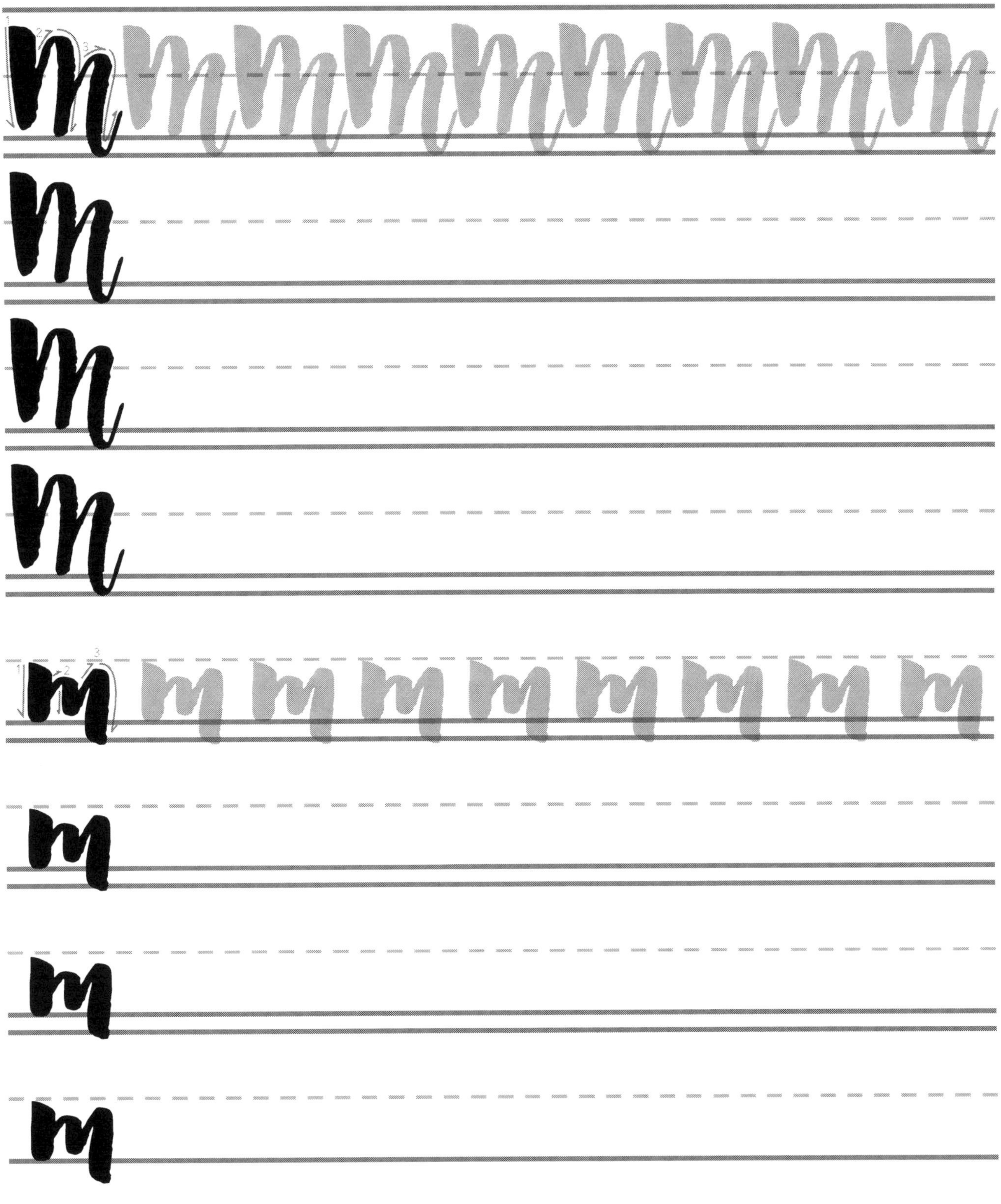

LET'S PRACTICE! TRACE THE FIRST ROW THEN TRY ON YOUR OWN

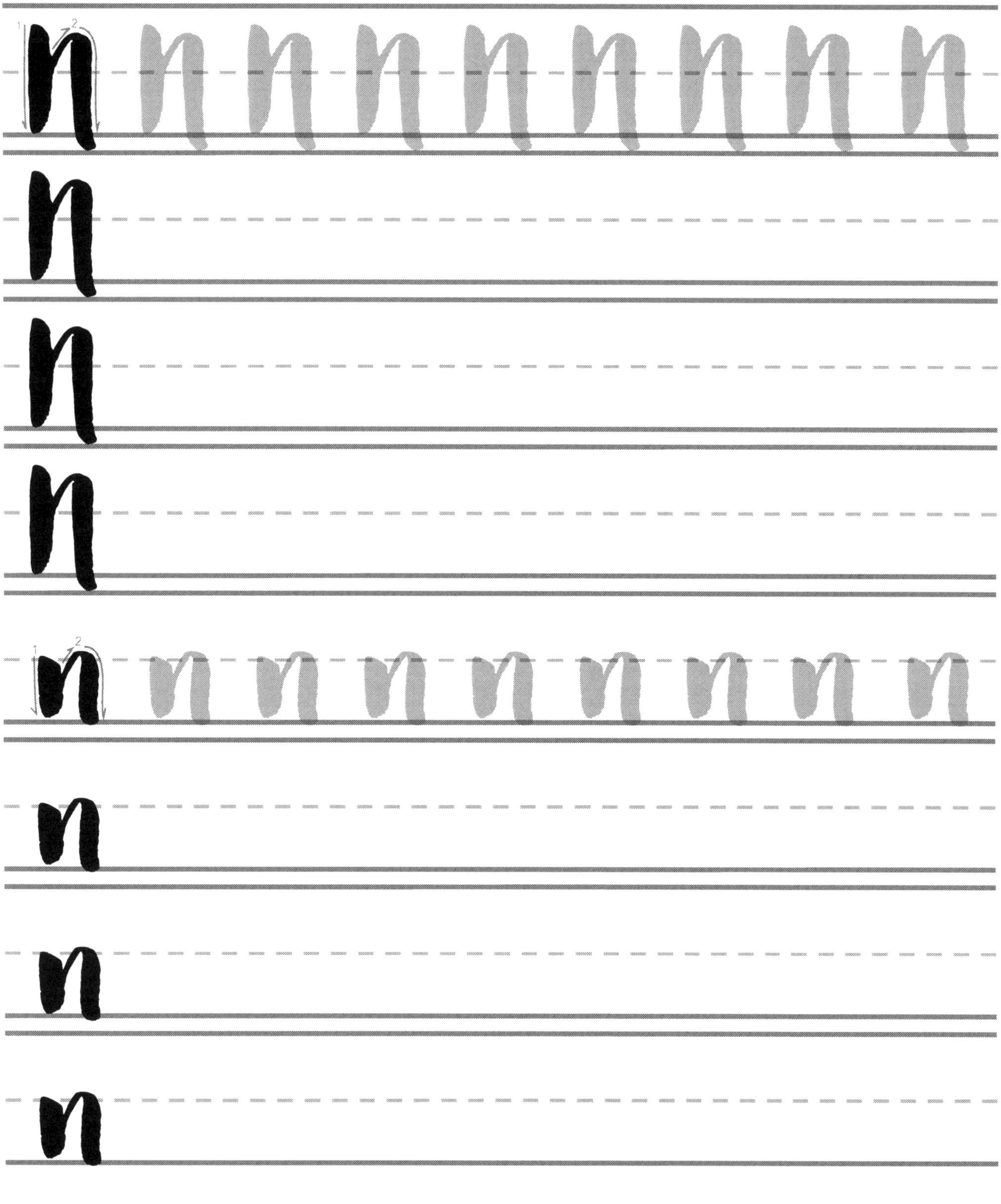

LET'S PRACTICE! TRACE THE FIRST ROW THEN TRY ON YOUR OWN

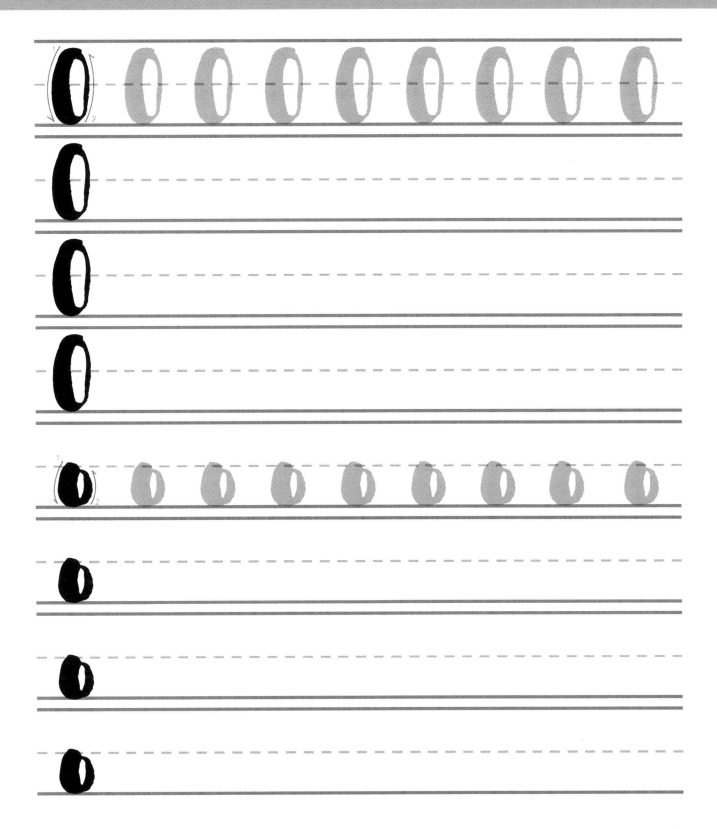

LET'S PRACTICE! TRACE THE FIRST ROW THEN TRY ON YOUR OWN

LET'S PRACTICE! TRACE THE FIRST ROW THEN TRY ON YOUR OWN

LET'S PRACTICE! TRACE THE FIRST ROW THEN TRY ON YOUR OWN

LET'S PRACTICE! TRACE THE FIRST ROW THEN TRY ON YOUR OWN

41

LET'S PRACTICE! TRACE THE FIRST ROW THEN TRY ON YOUR OWN

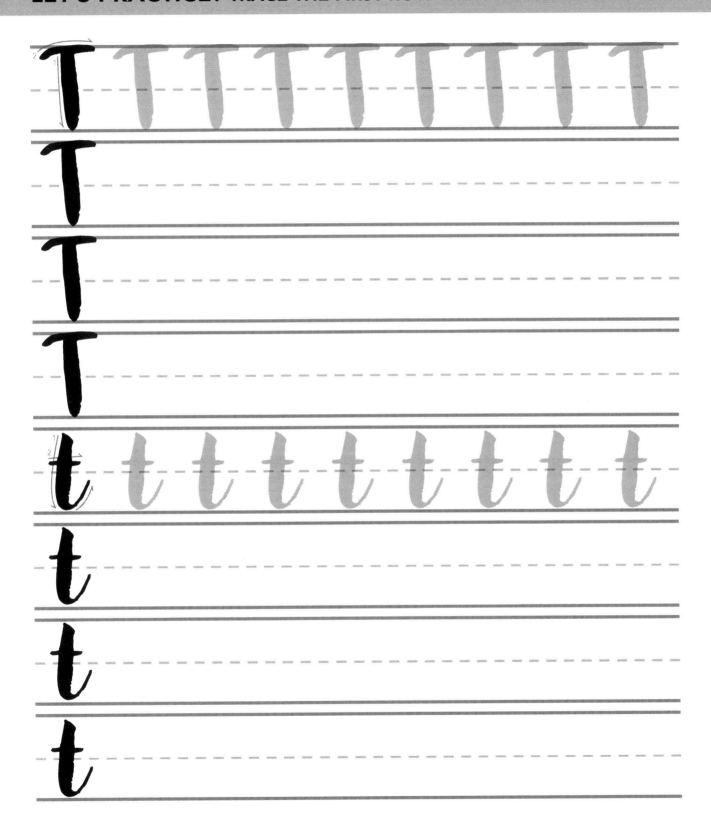

LET'S PRACTICE! TRACE THE FIRST ROW THEN TRY ON YOUR OWN

LET'S PRACTICE! TRACE THE FIRST ROW THEN TRY ON YOUR OWN

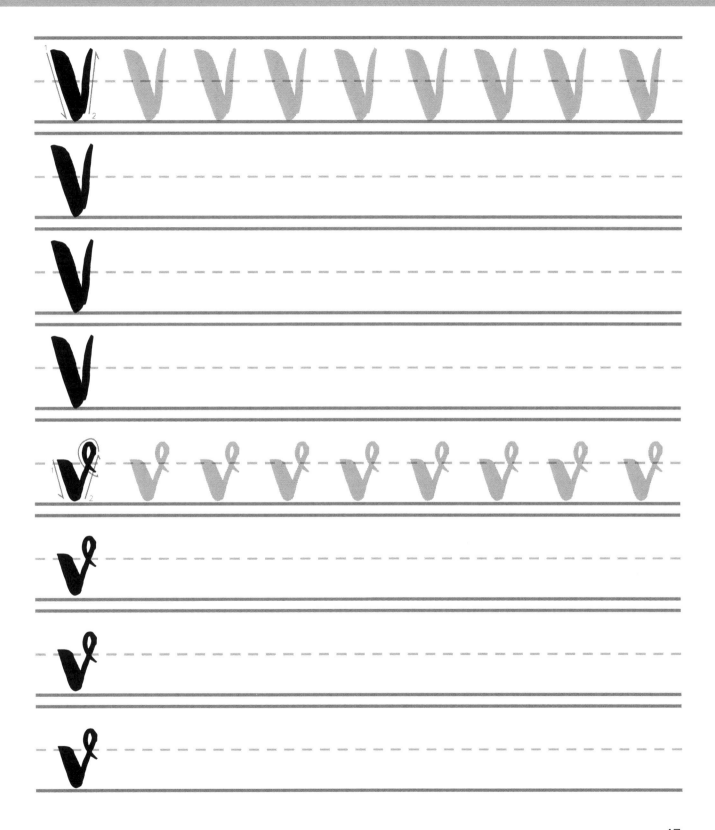

LET'S PRACTICE! TRACE THE FIRST ROW THEN TRY ON YOUR OWN

LET'S PRACTICE! TRACE THE FIRST ROW THEN TRY ON YOUR OWN

LET'S PRACTICE! TRACE THE FIRST ROW THEN TRY ON YOUR OWN

LET'S PRACTICE! TRACE THE FIRST ROW THEN TRY ON YOUR OWN

LET'S PRACTICE! TRACE THE FIRST WORD THEN TRY ON YOUR OWN

Beautiful

Beautiful

Beautiful

How fun!

How fun!

How fun!

LET'S PRACTICE! TRACE THE FIRST WORD THEN TRY ON YOUR OWN

Learning

Learning

Learning

Lovely

Lovely

Lovely

LET'S PRACTICE! TRACE THE FIRST WORD THEN TRY ON YOUR OWN

New Skills

New Skills

New Skills

Awesome

Awesome

Awesome

LET'S PRACTICE! TRACE THE FIRST WORD THEN TRY ON YOUR OWN

Keep it up

Keep it up

Keep it up

Amazing!

Amazing!

Amazing!

TRADITIONAL CALLIGRAPHY FONT - CAPITAL LETTERS

A B C D E F G H I
J K L M N O P Q
R S T U V W X Y Z

TRADITIONAL CALLIGRAPHY FONT - LOWERCASE LETTERS

a b c d e f g h i
j k l m n o p q r
s t u v w x y z

LET'S PRACTICE! TRACE THE FIRST ROW THEN TRY ON YOUR OWN

LET'S PRACTICE! TRACE THE FIRST ROW THEN TRY ON YOUR OWN

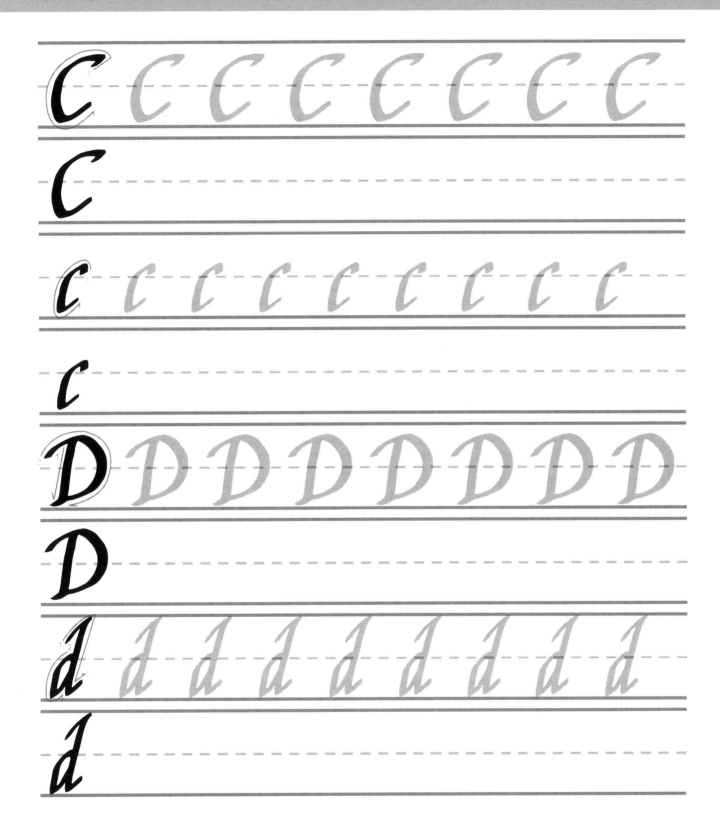

LET'S PRACTICE! TRACE THE FIRST ROW THEN TRY ON YOUR OWN

LET'S PRACTICE! TRACE THE FIRST ROW THEN TRY ON YOUR OWN

LET'S PRACTICE! TRACE THE FIRST ROW THEN TRY ON YOUR OWN

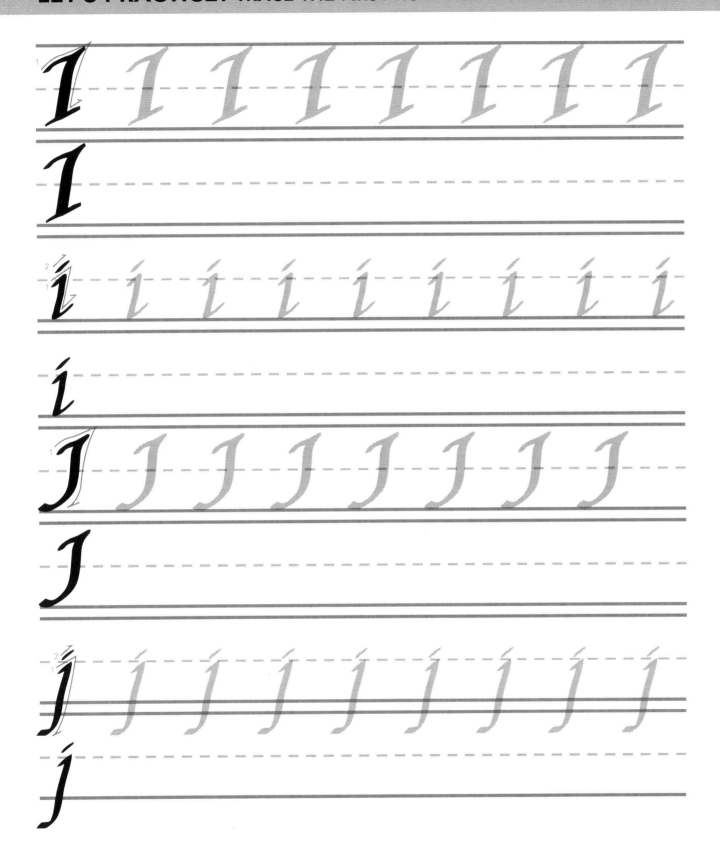

LET'S PRACTICE! TRACE THE FIRST ROW THEN TRY ON YOUR OWN

LET'S PRACTICE! TRACE THE FIRST ROW THEN TRY ON YOUR OWN

LET'S PRACTICE! TRACE THE FIRST ROW THEN TRY ON YOUR OWN

LET'S PRACTICE! TRACE THE FIRST ROW THEN TRY ON YOUR OWN

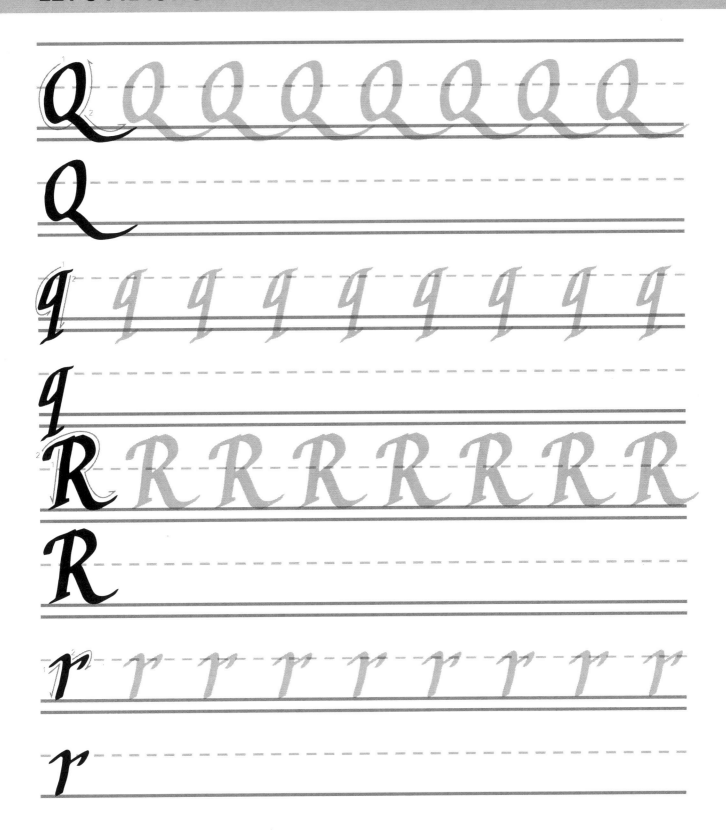

LET'S PRACTICE! TRACE THE FIRST ROW THEN TRY ON YOUR OWN

LET'S PRACTICE! TRACE THE FIRST ROW THEN TRY ON YOUR OWN

LET'S PRACTICE! TRACE THE FIRST ROW THEN TRY ON YOUR OWN

LET'S PRACTICE! TRACE THE FIRST ROW THEN TRY ON YOUR OWN

y y y y y y y y y

y

y y y y y y y y y

y

z z z z z z z z

z

z z z z z z z z z

z

LET'S PRACTICE! TRACE THE FIRST WORD THEN TRY ON YOUR OWN

Beautiful

Beautiful

Beautiful

How fun!

How fun!

How fun!

LET'S PRACTICE! TRACE THE FIRST WORD THEN TRY ON YOUR OWN

Learning

Learning

Learning

Lovely

Lovely

Lovely

LET'S PRACTICE! TRACE THE FIRST WORD THEN TRY ON YOUR OWN

New skills

New skills

New skills

Awesome

Awesome

Awesome

LET'S PRACTICE! TRACE THE FIRST WORD THEN TRY ON YOUR OWN

Keep it up

Keep it up

Keep it up

Amazing!

Amazing!

Amazing!

Made in the USA
Middletown, DE
02 November 2017